MEETING THE IGNOS

Susan T. Gardner and Arthur Wolf

Illustrated by Kezzia Crossley

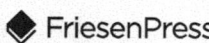 FriesenPress

Suite 300 - 990 Fort St
Victoria, BC, V8V 3K2
Canada

www.friesenpress.com

Copyright © 2018 by Susan T. Gardner and Arthur Wolf
First Edition — 2018

All rights reserved.

No part of this publication may be reproduced in any form, or by any means, electronic or mechanical, including photocopying, recording, or any information browsing, storage, or retrieval system, without permission in writing from FriesenPress.

ISBN
978-1-5255-1476-0 (Hardcover)
978-1-5255-1477-7 (Paperback)
978-1-5255-1478-4 (eBook)

1. PHILOSOPHY, ETHICS & MORAL PHILOSOPHY

Distributed to the trade by The Ingram Book Company

Immanuel is a fox—a red fox. He lives in Downtown Divercity, which is not far from and not unlike other towns. Immanuel is also a very smart fox. Not because he dresses smartly but because he takes **philosophy** class in school. Not everyone gets to take philosophy in school—just the ones who like to go on "*thinking adventures.*"

But lately Immanuel is out-and-out mad at philosophy, and here's why.

While you are on a philosophical thinking adventure, "reason should rule." So any opinion you have or any choice you make should be backed up by good reasons! This is especially important when you meet others on your trip. If you meet another, the only way to tell if you should follow the path that that person suggests is to listen to their reasons —*to really listen*. You could say it is not unlike "**putting yourself in the others' shoes.**" That doesn't mean you actually get into their shoes! That means that you get to see the world the way they see it. Well, at least a little bit. Once you have heard and can repeat the reasons for what others believe, then you must honestly try to figure out which opinion, or which choices, are the best. That is why thinking is never a lonely adventure. Together we can overcome our old careless ways of thinking, and dance towards **truth**. And *that* is what students in philosophy class do: they reason together.

But yesterday, Immanuel tried reasoning with Ignome. And the day before that, he tried reasoning with Ignogreed. And the day before that, he tried reasoning with Ignono, and the day before that, he overheard so much non-reasoning between Ignostatus and Ignofo that he couldn't think of anything to say. And the day before that, trying to reason with Ignotribus lead to a complete dead end. In all these instances, nobody seemed to be able to put on the other's shoes! Genuine **DIAlogue** seemed impossible. They were not exchanging ideas. Instead, they had parallel **MONOlogues**—everyone was talking, but no one was listening. Everyone seemed to be speaking into an **echo chamber**. They could only hear themselves, themselves, themselves!

Here is what happened when Immanuel met Ignome.

Ignome is a peacock who puts all his energy into making sure that everyone recognizes how wonderful and fabulous and beautiful he is. Yesterday, Ignome was involved in a discussion about the school play with his classmates. He was insisting, fairly strongly, that he get the lead part, when Immanuel happened to join the group.

"It is obvious that I, Ignome, should get the lead part!"

"But Ignome," Immanuel said, "you had the lead in the last play. Don't you think that Rory Rooster should have a turn?"

"No," said Ignome, "I am clearly more qualified. Just look at me!"

"But the part only says that the actor must be a bird, and Rory is as much a bird as you are."

"But," said Ignome, "I am a much more beautiful bird than Rory."

"You certainly are a beautiful bird, Ignome," said Immanuel, "but Rory has a lovely speaking voice, so he will be fine for the part."

"Are you telling me that I don't have a lovely voice?" screeched Ignome, puffing himself up to almost twice his size.

"No, no, no, that's not what I meant," said Immanuel. "Of course you have a lovely voice, Ignome; look what a beautiful job you did in the play last year. I meant that Rory would be fine for the part this year."

"Well, I will be *more than fine* for the part, so I should get the part," said Ignome, unfolding his tail with a grand swish. "Clearly when we pick individuals for parts in the play, we should pick the best, not just those who might be fine. We should pick the best bird for this part, and that is me!"

"But Ignome, don't you remember that last year the students voted for maximum inclusion in all school activities," said Immanuel, still hoping that Ignome would try to see his viewpoint. "That means we want as many people involved as possible."

"Don't be ridiculous," said Ignome with annoyance. "Everyone knows that they rigged the vote. And besides, if you go on Facebook, you will see that everyone wants **me** to take the lead part in the play."

It is all about me! It is all about me! thought Immanuel, trying to follow philosophy's suggestion that he should try to understand Ignome from his point of view. He wondered what it would be like to think about himself the whole day. He would say to everybody that he is the most fantabulous of all! And he could be the center of attention all the time. Maybe that is what its like in Ignome's shoes. But then he realized that not only was "me, me, me" not a very flattering way of thinking about Ignome, but that that was probably not what philosophy meant by suggesting that we should try and put ourselves into the shoes of others. But how could he get behind the "me-door"? That question weighed heavily on Immanuel's mind, particularly after his experience the day before.

The day before had been a bad one for Immanuel. He had gotten into a tangle with Ignogreed. Ignogreed was a magnificent pig who liked to collect stuff. The more stuff Ignogreed had, the better he felt. His favourite pastime was to trade his stuff with others, so that he could get even more stuff. Ignogreed's family also liked trading for stuff, but it was a habit that had unfortunate consequences. When the pig family first came to Downtown Divercity, they had the nicest piece of land in the neighbourhood. Trees, flowers, butterflies, bees, squirrels, and rabbits all around. There was even a pond where Henrietta Heron came to fish and discuss the day's events with Dorothy and Daniel Duck. Over time, though, the land changed. First they drained the pond so the pigs could have a bigger house. Then they cut the trees and exchanged the wood for stuff. Then they paved over the flower beds and built a garage to hold their stuff.

While this was happening, the butterflies, bees, squirrels, rabbits, birds, and ducks disappeared. The land began to look "stuffed." This upset the pigs a lot. They loved nature, so they exchanged a whole lot of their stuff for the large property that came up for sale next door. But before they knew it … before they could even seem to help themselves … that land, too, looked "stuffed." But then the piece of property on the other side of their home came up for sale.

All this had an **impact** on Ignogreed, or at least that is what his classmates thought. When he first came to school, he seemed pleased to be friends with everyone. But after a while, it seemed that Ignogreed only wanted to play with friends who also had lots of stuff. And before long, he and his "stuffy" buddies began to avoid the classmates who didn't have the same kinds of showy-off stuff that they did.

This sometimes led to disagreements, as it did about the school play. They had all agreed to put on a play. What they didn't agree on was the *reason* for putting on the play. Ignogreed and his buddies argued strongly that the money collected from the play should be used to upgrade the school gym. But many in the class wanted to give the money to the school in the next town, because they didn't have a gym at all.

When Immanuel heard both sides, he said to Ignogreed, "Don't you think it's important that all students have the same chance to do things in school as we do? Don't you think we should all have the same **opportunities** to be the best that we can be?"

"Opportunities are made, Immanuel," snapped Ignogreed, "not handed out on a silver platter. The people of this community paid to have our gym built. The community next door can do the same."

"But the families in the next community are not as rich as we are. They barely have enough to eat, let alone have the **luxury** of building a gym," said Immanuel, hoping to help Ignogreed understand how the students in the other town must feel.

"Well, just take a look at them. They are no different than we are, are they? So, why are they so poor? Well, I will tell you why," continued Ignogreed, not giving Immanuel a chance to respond. "They laze around waiting for hand-outs, that's why. If we give them hand-outs, they will never work, and we will have to give them hand-outs forever and ever. And that will actually be bad for them. That's the reason we shouldn't give them the money we make from the play. It would be bad for them!" said Ignogreed, looking around **smugly** at his classmates.

"But … but Ignogreed," said Immanuel, now seriously worried that his classmates might buy into Ignogreed's argument, "one of the reasons that the families in the next community are so poor is because the parents in those families never had the **opportunity** to go to school. And, *their* parents never had the opportunity to go to school either. It is like handing down a problem from one generation to the next. If we help to make their school better, maybe we can help break the cycle. This generation of youngsters will learn to love their school and do well. They will have a better chance to do well in life."

"What kind of a goody-two-shoes argument is that?" responded Ignogreed. "I know lots of people who had uneducated parents and did just fine in life, thank you very much. Besides, we all know that what's important in life is not where you start, but whether you have the *will to succeed*. And whether you have the will to succeed depends upon whether you get rewarded. Putting on this play is going to be hard. If we want to keep everyone excited about doing their best, they need to know that they will be rewarded with a better gym."

Immanuel knew that nothing he said would make any difference in this discussion. He was getting the feeling that Ignogreed was very determined to keep as much stuff as possible for the class. So determined even that this was a **fake dialogue**. Ignogreed rejected all the reasons that were offered against his position, without even considering if they might be stronger than the reaons he favoured.

That is when a thought crossed his mind. Ignogreed doesn't care about **truth**, which is the **ideal**, or "goal" toward which he and his classmates hoped to move, when they engaged in philosophical dialogue. He only cares about "stuff." As long as he had stuff, and lots of it, nothing else much mattered. He just wanted to feel stuffed!

Oh no, thought Immanuel, *that is not a very nice way to think about someone*. Surely, that is not what philosophy meant by **putting ourselves into the shoes of others**. But how could he get behind the "stuff-door"? That question weighed heavily on Immanuel's mind, particularly after his experience the day before.

The day before, Immanuel had had an encounter with Ignono. Ignono was a mule who seemed to go through life without a care in the world. Despite her happy-go-lucky attitude, Ignono made Immanuel very cross. Ignono had seen Willie Weasel beating up Immanuel's friend, Rachel Rabbit, but had done nothing about it.

"Why didn't you try to stop it?" asked Immanuel, barely able to contain his anger. "Or why didn't you at least go to get help?"

"I don't know. Why would I? It wasn't my problem, was it? Besides, I was too busy having a good time doing whatever I felt like doing at the moment," answered Ignono.

"But that is the problem, isn't it, Ignono? You are always doing just what you happen to feel like doing at the moment. Why are you always kind of lazing around?"

"I don't know," smiled Ignono, "it's fun."

"But why do you find it fun?" asked Immanuel with growing frustration.

"I don't know, it just is."

"But you must have a reason for doing what you do, Ignono. Not all Mules laze around, but you do, and you do it a lot. Now I am not saying that you have to be a 'busy bee mule,' but I am worried about the opposite. It must be having a negative **impact** on the way you think, on what you do, and, maybe more importantly, on what you don't do. So why do you do it?"

"I told you," said Ignono, still smiling, "I do it for fun."

"Something being fun is not a good reason for anything," replied Immanuel, trying out his new philosophy skills. "If someone came and beat you up just because they thought it was fun, that wouldn't be a very good reason, would it?"

"Look," said Ignono, with a tone that suggested she was finding this discussion boring, "from my point of view, everyone has their own reasons for doing what they do. Everyone has their own opinion, right? So nobody has the right to tell others that what they are doing is right or wrong. That is their opinion. Why should anyone listen to anyone else's opinion?"

Immanuel was about to explain that opinions are only as good as the reasons that back them up, and that we should listen to one another's *reasoned* opinions because they might be better than our own, when the thought occurred to him that reasoning wasn't important to Ignono. Ignono only cared if she liked or didn't like an idea. When it came to reasoning, there was nobody home.

Oh no, Immanuel thought, *that is not a very nice way to think about someone—as "empty-headed" or "a no-brainer."* That is not what philosophers meant when they said that you should try to put yourself into other people's shoes. But how could he get behind the "door to nowhere"? That question weighed heavily on Immanuel's mind, particularly after his experience the day before.

The day before Immanuel had overheard a discussion between Ignostatus and Ignofo. Ignostatus was a beautiful tiger; she had lots of friends. Who wouldn't want to be friends with a tiger, particularly since stripes were the in-thing in school these days? Being friends with Ignostatus meant that you were in the in-group, and that you were one of the important people. And what could be wrong with feeling important? That is precisely what Ignofo thought. Ignofo was a hyena, and she was always following Ignostatus around. In fact, it was Ignofo who started the stripe-trend in school. Even though she also had a striped coat, she always wore a striped cap that more closely matched the stripes of Ignostatus. In fact, Immanuel happened to be admiring Ignofo's cap when he overheard the following conversation.

"Ignofo, didn't I see you talking to Gary Goat on the way home yesterday?" asked Ignostatus of her friend. Without waiting for an answer, she continued, "Now, Ignofo, hanging around with that goat is definitely not a good idea. Look how scrawny he is, and he has those bucky-out teeth. In fact," said Ignostatus, with a belly laugh, "he is butt-ugly."

"Yeah, he is kinda ugly, isn't he?" replied Ignofo, with a kind of giggle that motivated her to rethink her friendship with Gary. "Come to think of it, he also has breath like a dung-heap," added Ignofo with an even louder laugh.

"Yeah, and he is always trying to show off in class by raising his hand," added Ignostatus. "Think about it—what would others think if they saw you with that nerd? Well, I will tell you what they would think," continued Ignostatus, without waiting for a response. "They would think that, deep down, you were a nerd-sympathizer!"

"A what?! Well, yeah, I guess so," added Ignofo, beginning to feel a bit concerned. "But I can't really avoid him, can I? He takes the same route home that I do."

"No problem, no problem. We can fix that," said Ignostatus, delighted with her new thought. "Every time we catch Gary alone, we will roar and scare the living daylights out of him. I promise, he will make sure to avoid you after that."

No sooner had Ignostatus said this, when Gary came around the corner. Seizing the opportunity, Ignostatus immediately let out a ferocious bellow that was accompanied by Ignofo's bark.

Immanuel watched in horror as Gary flew to safety inside the school. He could only imagine what Gary must have felt—seeing his friend Ignofo deliberately trying to frighten him.

I must try to talk to them, thought Immanuel. And that is when the thought crossed his mind. For Ignostatus, the only thing that mattered was how important she and her friends were. At first he had thought that there was nothing wrong with wanting to be important. But now he wondered if feeling important required feeling that others were *un*important. Trying to argue Ignostatus out of her need to put others down seemed as fruitless as arguing chickens out of their **pecking order**.

Oh no, thought Immanuel, *that is not a very nice way to think about others*. Surely that is not what philosophy meant by understanding the points of view of others. But how could he get behind the "status-door"?

And as for Ignofo, thought Immanuel, *she was just the rubber stamp of Ignostatus; in fact, maybe even worse*. At least Ignostatus believes in what she is doing; Ignofo is a follower—a kind of **scavenger** of Ignostatus's kill, all in the name of status!

Oh no, thought Immanuel, *that is not a very nice way to think about others*. Surely that is not what philosophy meant by understanding the points of view of others. But how could he get behind the "follower-door"? That question weighed heavily on Immanuel's mind, particularly after his experience the day before.

The day before, Immanuel had been in a discussion with Ignotribus. Ignotribus was a rat who thought he was pretty special, just because he was a rat! He thought that of all living creatures, rats were THE best. That is why Ignotribus didn't want to hang out with anybody except other rats. That seemed to be true of all the rats; they just wanted to hang out with each other. In fact, Ignotribus and his rat pack were so determined to hang out only with rats, that they set up a territory near the school playground. They put signs up that said "Rats Only! No Trespassing." That is how Immanuel happened to get into a discussion with Ignotribus.

Immanuel's friend, Beverly Beaver, had strayed into "Rat Territory" on her way to the river and the rat pack swarmed her. Though she was able to scamper away without too much injury, she begged Immanuel to talk to the rats. Being the runt of her litter, she was too small to fight for herself. She wanted Immanuel to convince the rats to let her pass through "Rat Territory" because the only other way to get to the river took three hours longer. And then it would be three hours back!

"No way, no way, no way," responded Ignotribus when Immanuel asked him if Beverly could have safe passage through Rat Territory. "Yuck! Yuck! Yuck! No way, no way, no way."

"But why?" asked Immanuel, shocked by the ugliness of Ignotribus's response.

"Beavers? Are you kidding me? Beavers—they are scum!"

"I don't understand," responded Immanuel. "Why are you saying that?"

"Get with the program, Buddy. Don't you know that all Beavers are dishonest? Give them half a chance, and they will rob you blind."

"I don't understand," repeated Immanuel. "Why are you saying that?"

"Because it is true, man. Ask anyone. Besides," continued Ignotribus, "we rats need to stick together. We are much better on our own. Look around you, man—rats are everywhere. We are on the verge of ruling the world. That is our fate; that is our right. King Rat; Rat is King!" Ignotribus threw up his paw in what looked like a military salute.

"But Ignotribus, Beverly not only *wouldn't* hurt a fly—she *couldn't* hurt a fly. You have nothing to be afraid of. I guarantee that she wouldn't try to rob any of you," said Immanuel.

"Yuck, yuck, yuck. No way, no way, no way," responded Ignotribus. "We won't be contaminated by a **snivelly**-faced whiner like your Beverly. Just the very fact that she can't stand up to us herself shows that she is a cowardly wimp. You should know, Immanuel," continued Ignotribus, in a more serious tone, "that we rats aren't in the least bit fooled by your namby-pamby **diversity**-talk stuff. That talk is just the talk of weaklings who are jealous of those of us who will ultimately rule; it is just a scheme to try to lessen our power. Don't you know that beavers cause flooding? In fact, many countries are trying to wipe out the **vermin**!"

That's rich, thought Immanuel, *the pot calling the kettle black*. But before he was able to think of a less hurtful response, a thought crossed his mind. For Ignotribus, the only thing that mattered was establishing the supremacy of the rat; what he thought of himself didn't seem to have anything to do with who *he* was and what *he* accomplished. He measured himself by rats *in general*. If they prospered, then he prospered. Trying to reason with Ignotribus that everyone prospers by **diversity** seemed pointless.

Oh no, thought Immanuel, *that is not a very nice way to think about someone.* Surely that is not what philosophy meant by putting ourselves into the shoes of others. But how could he get behind the "tribe-door"? That question weighed heavily on Immanuel's mind.

So all-in-all, Immanuel was feeling quite distressed. This was so unlike what he usually felt. Usually Immanuel was feeling very hopeful, and a lot of that hope came from what he learned in philosophy. In philosophy class, he and his mates looked at life's "big picture." They learned that the behaviour of all living things is **determined** by all the forces to which life is exposed: Attractive things (like food) pulled life towards them, while threatening things (like loud noises) pushed them away. And the same goes for friends, they pull you towards them. But scary things, like dark places, push you away. This push and pull of life often causes conflict, so without help, life could be "nasty, brutish, and short." This was the life of the jungle! But some bits of life found ways to pull themselves up from these natural life forces through the power of reason. Reason enables the development of **self-control** and protection against dangerous forces, so reasoning beings are able to cooperate and thrive as groups; they are also able to imagine what sorts of actions are required of them to become the people they hope to become. Immanuel learned that reasoning beings were **free** in a way non-reasoning beings are not.

Imagine, thought Immanuel, *I am in charge of me! So, though I might have a "natural" inclination to chase rabbits, I choose not to. And I like myself better that way.*

"But wait a minute," said Immanuel to his classmates, "I am beginning to think that there is something wrong with this picture! We have just figured out that reason helps us in becoming the kinds of people we want to become, but we also came to the conclusion that no one can reason all by themselves. **Rodin** got it wrong! I can't just put my paw to my chin and figure out what life is all about. I need to reason *with* other people! I need other people, because we can only go forward in reasoning by throwing out what is wrong. But we can't figure out how our own reasoning is wrong unless we expose what we think to others with different viewpoints. That means we all need to learn to **dialogue** with each other. What we have really learned is that "I am me only because of we!"

"But don't you see?" said Immanuel. "There is a **big fly in the ointment**. We keep stressing that we need to dialogue with others in order to ensure that our thinking is clear, and that clear thinking is necessary for us to really be in charge of who we are becoming, because otherwise our inclinations and forces in the environment just take over. But what do we do when other people don't want to, or just plain can't, dialogue with us?"

"Well," responded Rachel Rabbit, "maybe we could just double down on listening; we could listen carefully to ourselves so that we are talking in a way that the other might at least get a glimpse of what we think, and listen to the other in way that allows us to get a glimpse of their point of view. That way, even if the other is completely untouched by the interaction, we ourselves might be able to take a few baby steps closer to what is '**truthier**.'"

Immanuel felt discouraged. He imagined communication as two people meeting in the middle of a bridge. He knew that this did not mean that what happened in the middle was some kind of fifty-fifty compromise. The point of meeting in the middle was not to split the difference between **opposing viewpoints**. After all, if we split the bridge, we would all fall into the water! The point of meeting in the middle is just that: "meeting." By meeting, by truly understanding each others' reasoning, we might move closer to truth together.

Immanuel had indeed come across an enormous **fly in the ointment**—in fact he had come across several flies. Even if he was willing to walk to the middle of the bridge, the other might stay firmly on the other side—behind the doors that shielded "me," "greed," "empty," "status," "follower," or "tribe." The other might even trick him into leaving his own reasoning behind!

And so Immanuel brought the question he most eagerly wanted to explore to philosophy class; a big question. What do we do about all these closed doors? What do we do about all these closed minds?

"To begin with," responded Freddy Frog, "I think we need to figure out what we should FEEL about those who hide behind closed doors."

"Mad!" responded Immanuel firmly. "I just felt like kicking in those doors."

"But you can't, Immanuel," said Beverly Beaver sadly. "Doors to the mind are different from physical doors; they can only be opened from the inside."

"But if these doors are locked up tight, then those with shielded minds have locked themselves in. They have put themselves in prison," added Rachel Rabbit with a sense of amazement.

"Well, that sounds pretty SILLY to me," added Tiffany Tortoise in disgust.

"But we don't get mad at people who say silly things, do we?" asked Rachel Rabbit. "It's not like it's their fault. I don't think we should hold them **responsible** for saying silly things."

"Right," added Rory Rooster, "and if people are not **responsible**—if they can't really help it—then we can't get mad at them, can we? We don't get mad at dirt that turns into mud when it rains, do we? It just can't help itself."

"Maybe we should feel sorry for those who never had the kind of experience that helps to open the doors to their mind," said Freddy, wondering if he had finally answered his own question.

"Wait a minute," added Immanuel, "that can't be right. Thinking that others are just stupid bits of dirt doesn't seem like a very generous attitude. I don't think any of us would like to be viewed that way. I don't think that Ignostatus or Ignotribus would like to be thought of that way either. They would rather have us mad at them. Besides, these Ignos can be really mean. They can be hurtful. We can't just stand by feeling sorry for them while they **victimize** others, can we? If we are silent and don't do anything, aren't we part of the problem as well? We should stand up and act!"

"You're right, Immanuel, that doesn't seem right," responded Freddy Frog. "Ok, why don't we get back to your original question. You asked us what we thought we should do when someone that you are trying to dialogue with stays firmly on the other side of the bridge— behind the doors that shielded "me," "greed," "empty," "status," "follower," or "tribe." So, everyone, what should we do?"

Freddy Frog's question was met with group silence until Rachael Rabbit came to the rescue. "Ok," she said, "let's try to answer that question tomorrow. Maybe we should try to tackle each of the doors separately and see if we can come up with a good plan. Maybe we can find a way to open the door from both sides. Maybe we can find a way to be welcome. Freddy, you tackle 'me.' Beverly, you tackle 'greed.' Tiffany, you tackle 'empty.' Rory, you tackle 'status,' and I will tackle "follower." Immanuel, you tackle 'tribe.'"

"Yay," said Immanuel, "This will be fun. But now for some serious business. I have chocolate chip cookies in my philosophy backpack for everyone."

"Yay," responded the group enthusiastically. And with that, they headed for the locker room.

PHiLOSOPHiCAL DiCTiONARY

Dialogue–Dialogue is a conversation between two people who really listen and who could repeat the reasons for why the other believes what he or she believes. Dialogue is difficult when two people have different views. Try this out on your parents. Take a particular incident about which you disagreed, say, whether or not you should finish all your homework before being allowed to watch TV (but make it real). You give all the reasons for why you think you shouldn't have had to complete your homework. Then ask them to repeat what you just said. Make sure they get it right. Then they get to say why they think you should have completed your homework. Then you have to repeat all the reasons why they thought you should have completed your homework. They get to decide if you understood their position correctly. Now you should discuss together which side had the "weaker" reasons and why. In dialogue, each participant should be able to *feel* what it is like to be the other person, which also means that you have to be sensitive to the context of that other; you have to imagine yourself in the other's shoes. See below: **Putting yourself in another's shoes.**

Diversity–In nature, an environment with many different kinds of plants—an environment with a high level of diversity—is considered healthy. This is so because different plants bring different benefits. Some have deep roots and so can stop the water from running away; some are good at creating nutrients or foods for the soil, and so on. Humans, too, benefit from living in a diverse environment for the same reason. But humans have a hard time seeing the benefits of diversity because they are more comfortable being with others who are exactly like they are. People who are the same are more predictable. So, aside from being beneficial, diversity has its challenges. Does your classroom have a high level of diversity? Do you mostly hang out with others who are just like you? Why do you think it is difficult to hang out with others who are not like you? Why not give yourself a challenge and try to make friends with someone who is not at all like you?

Determined–If a thing is determined, it means it has no choice. The earth is determined to revolve around the sun. It has no choice. Flowers are determined to bend toward the sun. They have no choice. Rocks roll down hill. They have no choice. Animals are determined by their biology to seek food. They have no choice. But because you are a self-conscious, rational, language-using person, you have gained the capacity for **self-control** (see below). You can decide not to eat a cookie even if your body wants it. Because you are *not* determined (at least not completely), you are **responsible** (at least partly; see below) for the choices that you make. Immanuel thinks that being responsible is the best thing ever. He is glad that he is not determined like most other animals. Do you agree?

Echo chamber–An echo chamber is an enclosed space in which sounds bounce off walls, and often become louder as a result. This also describes what happens when people don't listen to one another. Words just bounce around without actually entering minds, and they often become louder in the process. Have you ever found yourself not listening, so that someone else's words just bounce back at them?

Have you ever felt that people aren't listening to you? Does your voice get louder when people don't listen? Does this help?

Fake dialogue–see **echo chamber** above.

Fly in the ointment–To say that there is a "fly in the ointment" means that you have discovered some kind of problem or unpleasantness in a situation that would otherwise be fine. So you might say "I am so glad that we are going to Grandma's house. The only fly in the ointment is that I have to wear that scratchy outfit." For Immanuel, a fly in the ointment becomes evident when he realizes that, even though he might be willing to reason with others, the other might not be willing or able to reason with him. For **dialogue** to take place (see above), both must be willing. Have you ever come across this fly in the ointment?

Free–There are two main uses of the word "free" in philosophy. Free can mean "lack of constraint"–that there is nothing stopping you from doing what you want to do. If you lived in a world in which there were no rules, you would be free in that sense. Being free in that sense, though, is not something to be proud of. Bugs are free to fly around, and we don't admire them for that. But, there is another, more positive way, in which you can be free. You can control your own actions, and, because of that, you are free to create the kind of person you want to become. Bugs can't do that. Think about these two kinds of freedom: the bug kind and the human kind. Have you ever found yourself wishing that you had more "bug freedom"? Have you ever wished that you didn't have to follow rules? What rules do you wish you didn't have to follow? Are there some rules that actually increase your freedom? Are there some rules that help you gain **self-control** (see below) so that you are more free to become the person you want to be? If so, that means that there are some rules that deny some kinds of "bug freedom," but which help the human kind of freedom to grow. Which rules are those?

Ideal–An ideal is an imagined goal that guides our behaviour, but is something that we can never fully achieve. Thus, though we might have an ideal of clean clothes, we know, from the start, that clothes can never be perfectly clean. Still, an ideal is very useful in letting us know when we go too far astray. We know, for example, that very dirty clothes are not close to the ideal of clean. You can also have ideals about the kind of person you want to be every day of your life. If you have ideals, that will help to warn you when you are going astray. If one of your ideals is to be fair, that will help you to share during those times when you are thinking that it is actually not much fun to share. The ideal of truth is also just an ideal. In most instances, we can never get to perfect **truth** (see below), but the ideal can help us avoid what is untrue—like dirty clothes.

Igno–You will see that there are a number of characters in this adventure whose names begin with "Igno." While this prefix refers to the word "ignorant," it does not refer to how ignorant is usually meant. People usually think of "ignorant" as "lacking in knowledge." Thus, someone might say that, compared to adults, children are ignorant. This is *not* how the term is being used here. Here, the term "ignorant" is being used to refer to a *refusal to try to really see why others think differently*; it is a refusal to engage in genuine **dialogue**; it is a refusal to reflect on the reasons for

opposing points of view. So, if Sally has lots and lots of toys, and someone suggests that she should share them but she refuses to really listen to their reasons, she could be called "Ignogreed" because her greed prevents her from listening to an opposing viewpoint. Lots of adults are "Ignos," so even if they have lots and lots of knowledge, they could still be "an Igno" compared to a child who really tries to listen to opposing viewpoints. The whole point of this adventure with Immanuel is to help you avoid being or becoming "an Igno." This will be better for you because listening to different points of view is the only way that you can figure out what is **true** (see below). It will also be better for the whole world because, if none of us are Ignos, all of us together will be able to figure out the best ways to live together, to say nothing of the fact that it is hard to be really mean to someone else when you really understand them.

Impact–If something has an impact, it has an effect; it causes something else to happen. Ignogreed was surrounded by "stuff" all the time. Because of that, he came to really love having stuff and getting stuff. Are you surrounded by "stuff"? Do you think it has an impact on you?

Luxury–If you have luxuries, you have more than you need. Do you have any luxuries? Immanuel seems to think that, if his school has luxuries, like a gym, they should share. Do you have any luxuries that you think you should share?

Monologue–A monologue is a long speech by one person. Try it out. Pick a topic like *why you don't like to clean your room*, and try giving a 3-minute monologue to your mother about why you don't like to clean your room. Ask her to time it. You will see that it is hard to give a monologue when everyone else is silent. But when other people are talking, it is easy to give a monologue: you just allow others to interrupt from time to time, and then keep on going with what you were saying. That is often how two people "talk together" (see **fake dialogue** above): they each give a monologue, but allow themselves to be interrupted from time to time by the monologue of the other. So each is just talking (giving a monologue) and no one is listening. You can tell if you are really listening by shutting down your monologue and trying, instead, to repeat what the other person is saying. Try it out. The next time you have a disagreement with someone, try to repeat *what* you think they are saying and *why* they are saying it. You may find that the other person is completely surprised. Most people are used to engaging in group monologues and can be quite shocked when someone actually listens.

Opportunity–To have an opportunity is to have a chance to do things. Some children in the world have the opportunity to go to school; some children do not. Some children have the opportunity to play sports, to read books, to use computers. Some children do not. How important is it to have such opportunities? What, if anything, should you do or feel if others don't have the same opportunities that you have?

Opposing viewpoints–If you think that we should not invite Sally to the party but I think we should, that means we have opposing viewpoints. The word "opposing" comes from the word "opposite." When Immanuel imagines that **dialogue** between people with opposing views is like *meeting in the middle of the bridge,* he is not imagining that somehow we can both get our way, or that we can have a fifty-fifty split: that we might decide, for example, to invite Sally to the party and then send her home halfway through. What he is imagining is that we both listen to the reasons for why we see the situation differently. Maybe Sally has said really mean things about you behind your back, so inviting her to the party would ruin it for you. Maybe I think Sally should come to the party because everyone else in the class has been invited, and not inviting her would make us look really mean. So maybe together we decide that you should go and talk to Sally and tell her that you know what she has been saying behind your back, and then ask her if there is some way that both of you can be nice to each other so that you both can enjoy being at the party. Remember that such **dialogue** (see above) doesn't always result in a solution; however, you never know unless you try. Dialogue is an **ideal** (see above).

Pecking order–Flocks of chickens create patterns of behaviour that is ordered like a ladder: those on the higher rungs know they can peck those on the lower rungs without fear of being pecked in return. Those on the lower rungs just submit to pecking from those higher up. Humans organize themselves in the same way—particularly in the work environment. The boss can criticize those who work for him, while they cannot criticize him back. In informal social groups, like friends and acquaintances, there are also often bosses who treat others as if they were less important. Do you know anyone amongst your friends who seems to be the boss? Are you often the boss? How easy do you think it would be for bosses and non-bosses to change places? Or is it a very firm "**pecking order**"? Is this a good way to be?

Philosophy–A philosopher is someone who is *wise*. Being *wise* is different from being *intelligent*. A *wise* person is someone who is concerned about her own actions, and how they add up to create a good life. An *intelligent* person might know lots of stuff, like how to write the best computer program ever (!), but she might still mess up her life. Philosophers usually don't get caught up in those kinds of smarty-pants competitions; philosophers are too concerned about the big-picture questions of *how we ought to live* and *what is a good life*. But because the big picture can only be created by small bits, the questions that philosophers ask often seem small and unimportant to those who don't understand that a life is made up of every single action that a person does or does not do. Because Immanuel is a philosopher, he is concerned by what might seem like small, even unimportant questions, like whether Ignome should let Rory Rooster have the lead part in the play, or whether Ignono should have tried to stop Willie Weasel from beating up Rachel Rabbit. So, if you told Immanuel that you wanted to be a person who was fair, kind, and reasonable (the big picture), he would say that you need to reflect upon small questions like whether or not it's fair if a child doesn't clean her room, or whether it is unkind for a child to make a fuss about going to bed, or whether there are times when it is OK not to share your toys, and so on. In *Philosophy for Children* classes, these are the sorts of questions that might be tackled.

Putting yourself in another's shoes—The funny thing about minds is that they are invisible. When you see another human, all you see is a body. For all you know, they could be robots. Because you can't see someone else's mind, the only way to understand what is going on in there, is through **dialogue** (see above). You have to keep asking them questions and really listening to their answers to know how that other person sees the world; you have to try to imagine what it would be like to be them. This is called "putting yourself in another's shoes." It could also be called "putting on someone else's glasses." Just imagine how exciting life would be if you could see it through all kinds of different lenses. And besides, your glasses might be cloudy or filled with cracks, so borrowing other people's glasses may help you see more clearly. Try this out. If you have a parent who works, ask them what it is like to do the work they do. What do they like about it? What do they not like about it? Do they think you would like it? If so, why? If not, why not? Try to imagine what it would be like to be them going off to work in the morning. Try putting it into words and see how close you can get.

Responsible–To say that someone is responsible is to say that they can be blamed or praised. We only hold those who have some kind of **self-control** (see below) as responsible. You don't hold an apple responsible when it falls from a tree and bonks you on the head. But you would hold your classmate responsible for bonking you on the head. Most of us don't like to be held responsible when we do bad things. Most of us don't like to be blamed, and none of us like to be punished. But we all like to be praised. The problem is you can't have one without the other. You need to remember that if someone praises you **or** blames you, that means that they believe that you are responsible for what you did, and that means that they see you as **free** (see above) or in control of what you did. Being seen as free to control your actions is the best compliment of all. Remember we don't hold bugs responsible for what they do. So the person who is blaming you, doesn't see you as a bug. If they *didn't* hold you responsible, it's bug-city for you!

Rodin–Auguste Rodin was a French Sculptor who died in 1917. One of his famous sculptures is called *The Thinker* (look it up on the net). When people think of "philosophers," they often think of them as "great thinkers," and that thinking is best done alone—just as *The Thinker* is alone in the sculpture. Although, certainly, some good thinking can be done on your own, the best thinking needs to be done with others. That is because all of us have difficulty seeing the faults in our own reasoning; that is why the best thinking requires that we **dialogue** (see above) with others.

Scavenger–When talking of animals, a scavenger refers to a creature that feeds on what is already dead—perhaps something killed by another. Hyenas feed on the carcasses of animals killed by their more powerful cousins, like lions. In this story, Ignofo is called a scavenger because she isn't a "bully" on her own. She Is a **fo**llower. She feeds off the **opportunities** (see above) that Ignostatus creates—in this case, joining in to scare Gary Goat. One way to be a scavenger in the human world, is to be part of group that makes life difficult for those not in the group. Scavengers feed off the energy and protection of the group, and they get rewarded by thinking that they are better than those who are not in the group. Do you know any scavengers? Should we all act like Gary Goat when faced with scavengers and bullies?

Self-control–Bodies have minds of their own. If you put meat in front of a dog, the dog's body will run to it and gobble it all up. If there are lots of dogs, they will fight over the meat. But if your teacher puts a plate of cookies in front of you and your classmates, you are able to prevent yourself from pouncing on the cookies and gobbling them all up. That is because you are able to reason with yourself and imagine what a mess it would be if everyone did that. That is what is called "self-control"; your "self" controls your body. We all lose self-control from time-to-time. Have you ever shouted at someone, when maybe you shouldn't have, and then thinking back, wondered why you did that? That was your body in control, not yourself. That's what could be called an "oops moment." If you say, "Oops, I shouldn't have done that. Sorry," that shows that it was not really "you" who was mean, it was your body. And the "sorry" indicates that you are going to try and get that body of yours under control. Describe a time when you lost self-control? What did you do afterwards? What should you have done afterwards? Remember, though, that sometimes someone can have too much self-control, like when they don't let themselves cry when it is perfectly alright or even better to cry. Has that ever happened to you?

Smug (looking around smugly)—If you look around smugly like Ignogreed did, you would look around as if you are smarter or better than everyone else. Can you try looking around smugly? Do you know anyone who ever looks that way?

Snivel—To snivel is to make a kind of snuffling noise through the nose, as you do when you are crying. If someone says "don't snivel," they are suggesting that you are acting like a baby—that you are being a whiner. When Ignotribus is referring to Beverly Beaver as a "snivelly faced whiner," it is an insult that suggests that she should not be respected because she can't fight her own battles. She's a cry-baby.

Have you ever called someone a "cry-baby"? Have you ever been called a "cry-baby"? Is it OK to be a cry-baby? If so, why? If not, why not?

True/truth—When someone, like Ignotribus, makes a claim, like "we should keep non-rats out of our territory," you have to decide whether to believe it or not; you have to decide whether it is true or false. You should only believe that a claim is true after you have carefully examined all the reasons and evidence that support its truth—AND—all the reasons and evidence that suggest that it is false. Scientists approach truth through the backdoor. They first try to show that a claim is false, and if they cannot show that it is false, then they say that we should believe it is true—*until* someone can show that it is false. So, if a scientist wants to investigate whether a drug cures a disease, she first tries to show that it does not work. This is called the "null hypothesis." If she cannot show that the drug does not work, then she will say that we should believe that it is true that the drug works—*until* someone else can show that it does not, or until someone comes up with a better drug. Try it out. Take something that you believe to be true, for example you might believe that it is true that Sally is not someone you want to be friends with. Then try to prove its opposite. Think of all the reasons why you might want to be friends with Sally. If you can think up reasons for why you might want to be friends with Sally, and they are not weaker than the reasons for why you don't want to be friends with Sally, then, at least for the time being, you should **not** believe that it is **true** that Sally is not someone you want to be friends with.

Truthier–"Truthier" is not really a word, but it should be. And here's why. If you take a look at how truth was explained above, you will see that it makes sense to believe that a claim is true if it seems *better than all other possibilities*. So what we usually mean when we say that a claim is "true" is that it is "truthier" than other alternatives, but that, later on, we may find that different possibilities are even more "truthier." The problem with saying that something is true, is that we usually believe that true is a *forever term*. When we use the term "true," we often think that our quest has come to an end because we have found "**The** Truth." So, instead of saying that a claim is true, if we said that it is truthier, that would remind us that claims to truth always depend on the number of other imagined possibilities to which it is compared. And it would remind us that we should keep on trying to imagine better ways to do things and better ways to be. Try it out some time. If someone makes a claim, any claim (like "I think Sally is a mean person"), if you can't think of another way of looking at the situation, just say "I think that that is truthier" instead of saying "I think that's true." See what kind of discussion emerges. (Note, though, that there are some claims that are forever true, like $2 + 2 = 4$.)

Vermin–Vermin is usually taken to refer to small disgusting creatures that are difficult to control, like rats or cockroaches. But people sometimes use the term to refer to each other. When people go to war against one another, they usually call the other side by a name like "vermin" or "cockroaches," so that it makes it easier to kill the "enemy." If they saw the enemy as humans, just like us, it would be harder to do them harm. Have you ever used a nick-name for people you don't like? Have others ever used a nick-name for you? Try and think of some nick-names that could be either positive or negative and then reflect on how that might change behaviour.

Victimize–A victim is someone who has been harmed, so the word "victimize" means to harm someone. Immanuel is saying that he and his friends should not stand silently by while bullies harm others. Do you agree? Do you ever victimize others? Do you know anyone who does? What should you do?

PARENT/TEACHER GUIDE FOR *MEETING THE IGNOS.*

Our goal for our children is that they be "reasonable."[1] "Reasonable" means not only being able to give reasons for what one believes and does, but also, to listen to and understand the viewpoints of those who think differently, and thereafter, to reason together with those others, so as to overcome brittle, often inaccurate, ways of thinking. By doing this, our children's lives will be enormously enriched, as will the lives of all with whom they come into contact.

One way to motivate youngsters to adopt the goal of being "reasonable" is to give them a peek at what "unreasonable" looks like. *Meeting the Ignos* does just that: it gives youngsters a glimpse at some of the many forms that "unreasonable" can take. Getting a look at "unreasonable" also helps refine the ideal of "reasonable," so that it has more magnetic power. Just as one might, in teaching skiing, show a video of skier falling because her weight was too far back, so, when teaching reasoning, it is helpful to show what happens when you don't listen to, and reason, with others.

"Igno forces" live in all of us to one degree or another. We are all prone to narcissism, greed, laziness, status-seeking, conformity, and tribal tendencies. If we understand how these forces manifest themselves and become obstacles to clear thinking, we will be better able to overcome them when they start to get in the way of who it is that we want to become.

A companion goal to *Meeting the Ignos* is to show that even reasonable people can sometimes be utterly at a loss when confronted with those who cannot or will not engage in an authentic reasoning process, usually because of steel-door biases. In such instances, the result may be that reasonable individuals may begin to lose faith in "reason as a way of life" due to its seeming inadequacy in such situations. In order to prevent this loss of faith, we must alert our youngsters to the fact that they will inevitably "meet the ignos" (those who do not want to, or are incapable of, reflecting on points of view that are different from their own). They must know that such communicative impasses do not indicate an inadequacy on their part, nor do they undermine the value of being a reasonable person when circumstances warrant. Viewing the different exchanges between Immanuel and the various Ignos will show youngsters that even a reasonable, well-meaning child (fox) can be utterly at a loss when attempting to deal with those who refuse to genuinely reflect on the merits of opposing viewpoints.

Our hope is that adults will use this book to create opportunities to reason with youngsters; more specifically, to question youngsters if they have ever encountered the sort of issues that Immanuel faces, and if so, to reason together about how best to handle them. Who knows? Enticing strategies may emerge. A more over-arching hope, however, is that adults will reason together with youngsters about how best to avoid becoming an Igno, and, in so doing, create a life-long habit of reasoning with others through life's challenges.

We suggest that this book be used as a companion over many days or sessions. The entire book and the dictionary could be read and discussed to begin with. On subsequent days, we suggest that each Igno be discussed separately, and that considerable time be devoted to carrying out some of the activities offered below. We suggest, too, that should you have the opportunity to enroll your children in a *Philosophy for Children* program (run in some 60 countries around the world and represented on the website of the *International Council for Philosophical Inquiry with Children* at http://icpic.org), seize it! Not only will your child, as an individual, benefit enormously, but the entire world benefits as each child adopts a *dialogical mode of being*, and in so doing, learns to take some control over her own destiny by carefully (and, hopefully, playfully) reflecting with others on the kind of person she wants to become, and the kind of world she wants to help create, as she makes her way along life's path.

NOTE ABOUT THE TITLE

It may be evident that the term "igno" is borrowed from the word "ignorant" and, as such, may seem odd to some, as the term is more often used to refer to someone who is unintelligent or unknowing is some way. This is **not** how the term is being employed here. Rather, the term is being used specifically to refer to an inability to seriously reflect on the merits of the views that are opposed to one's own; it is being used to refer to someone with a steel-door bias. To avoid being an "igno," one must be open and sensitive to another person's expression of their own thoughts, and then be willing to engage with them. In philosophical circles, this reflects a movement away from the notion of rationality as something that can be achieved by a solitary thinker (as depicted by Rodin's *The Thinker* and famously by Descartes and Kant) and more toward rationality as a dialogical process (as described by Habermas and Lipman). Another way of putting this is to say that none of us should presume that we are "rational" or "reasonable" unless we are prepared to reflect on the potential flaws and gaps in own reasoning. And, due to our own biases, usually others are in a much better position to see those flaws than we are. In other words, we can *only* be intelligent, rational, or reasonable by being open to the viewpoints of others; otherwise, we are "ignos."

SUGGESTIONS FOR DISCUSSION WITH AND BETWEEN CHILDREN

If you undertake reasonable discussions with children, you should try to reinforce the value of *reasoning together* by *reasoning together* on questions that arise through the journey of meeting the Ignos. Always keep in mind that the goal is NOT to INCULCATE values (no matter how tempting), such as the values of unselfishness or generosity or humility, as values are rarely stable or flexible unless they are voluntarily accepted or "introjected" through the glue of reason—that is, by discovering the value of those values by reasoning it out. Also, in order to keep reasoning for "depth," it is important to keep probing in the face of conversation-stopping politically correct or "expected" responses. So if a child says about Ignome that obviously he is bad because no one should insist on always having the lead part in the play, a series of genuine questions would be appropriate: Why is that bad? Wouldn't it actually be a good idea if we could always get our own way? Why is Immanuel so sure that Ignome is wrong? As well, try to get comfortable with using this Igno adventure as merely a springboard to create your own adventures in reasoning with your children. Once you start to become comfortable with the kind of questioning strategies suggested, you will find they apply to many other situations as well.

So, let us now move to a more precise guide by focusing on the individual characters that we encountered in our adventure of *Meeting the Ignos.*

IGNOME

All of us are inclined to lash out at those who have an insatiable need to be the center of attention. How could we not when confronted with a narcissist who is devoid of interest in others, has an elevated sense of entitlement, and little capacity to listen.[2] On the other hand, we may be able to temper our annoyance, somewhat, by remembering that these are not happy folks. Their lack of self-knowledge (depth) tends to result in a loss of joy, spontaneity, trust, and intimacy. And despite their "me, me, me" armor, we ought not to give up immediately on the possibility of communication. Neuroscience has shown that *how* we talk to one another actually changes the brain.[3] So, sometimes, listening so that the other actually "feels" heard, creates an emotional shift that opens up to the possibility of the other listening to you in return; it creates an entrance into each other's world.

We need to remember, though, to keep our expectations in check, and to always be prepared to take a stand against abuse and control by utilizing an authentic and assertive voice. And, we need to remember also that, precisely because narcissism is so problematic once established, prevention is a must. It is a pressing responsibility, in other words, that we help our kids avoid symptoms of narcissism (a characteristic now rampant in college students and young adults) by helping them learn to be accountable without feeling flawed and damaged. Clearly, if one feels great pressure to be perfect, one will be preoccupied with the self. So flaws, mistakes and shortcomings should be welcomed as signs of learning (oops!). And in support of the credibility of this view, it is imperative that we adults model the fact that we ourselves are comfortable with being "perfectly imperfect."

On the other hand, we need also to remember that the opposite extreme is equally damning. If you do not hold your children sufficiently accountable, they will fail to see themselves mirrored in your reactions, and hence fail to grasp that they, as individuals, are responsible agents. The problem with that is that, if there are no other individuals on stage, then the stage is all narcissistically theirs. It is all a fine balance.

Lastly, but above all, we need to listen to our children so that they feel "felt." It is in within the glow of visibility that their worries about "the self" diminish, and, as a result, they become more comfortable travelling into the self of another.

Questions to ask your kids

Q. Do you know anyone who acts like Ignome in school? [Ask them to describe the situation.]

Q. Why do you think that person behaves in that way?

Q. How do you react? Why?

Q. What would be the best way to react? Why?

Q. What kind of attention does this person need?

Q. Do you sometimes need this kind of attention?

Q. Can you think of reasons why, and why not, this kind of attention can be justified?

Activity

Together with a friend or parent write down what you sometimes seek attention for. Discuss with each other why you do that. Next write down your perfect self as you would like to present it. Discuss and compare. Finally, write down your worst self and have fun!

Think of one particular Ignome scenario. Describe it and then write down at least three possible responses. Now have fun and try acting them out together.

IGNOGREED

It is absolutely natural for all of us to want at least as much stuff as the other guy. Even animals strenuously object to getting less than the other.[4] This tendency to accumulate more and more stuff, however, is exacerbated beyond all need by the might of corporate power and marketing strategies. Just to remind us what we are up against, it is helpful to reflect upon the fact that, out of the fifteen companies/governments with the largest budgets, six are governments and nine are corporations.[5] Also, of the 100 largest economies in the world, fifty-one are global corporations and only forty-nine are countries.

The big danger that "addiction to stuff" poses is that (1) we lose sight of the distinction between stuff and happiness (we forget that more of one does not produce more of the other), and therefore (2) we are so busy listening to "gimme gimme gimme," that we have little time to seriously exercise our capacity to self-create. In other words, we become "one-dimensional;"[6] We come to think that collecting stuff is what life is all about.

One way to help our youngsters create another dimension is by asking them first to imagine the best kind of person they can think of, and then ask them to describe what they think that person would want, and why. In this way, when they are in the "I want that stuff" dimension, they may be able to jump to the "reasoning" dimension and ask themselves *why* they want that stuff, and if they really *want to want* that stuff.[7] And, of course, it is by engaging youngsters in reason-giving in all aspects of their lives that this dimension is solidified. Once they come to value reasoning, and value themselves and others as "reasoning beings," the value of being "over-stuffed" will lose its sheen.

Questions to ask your kids

Q. Do you know somebody in school who is an Ignogreed?

Q. How do you recognize somebody like that? What are the signs?

Q. What would you be devastated about if you lost it? Why?

Q. What is the difference between something you want and something you need?

Q. What counts as success? What does your life have to be like in order to think of it as a success? Why?

Q. If a neighbour has a bigger house, does that mean they have a better life? Why?

Q. Do you think that Ignogreed is right when he says that people are always more excited about, and put more effort into, activities for which there is an external reward?

Q. Would you care if there were nothing but plastic trees and plastic flowers? Why?

Q. Would you care if someday soon there were no tigers left in the wild? Why?

Activity

Collect five things you really wanted—that is, things you already have and got because you wanted them. Now discuss why you wanted them and write down the reasons. Next, order them according to the extent to which you need them. Again, think of reasons why and compare with your "wants" list. You might want to ask your siblings and parents to do the same, and compare lists. Collect five things that you once really wanted but that you don't want now. Why did you want those things? Did you have "good reasons" for wanting those things?

IGNONO

We are all confronted with the actions of others that ring warning bells. These situations are a challenge. Do we or do we not get involved? For Ignonos, the answer is always "no." The lyrics to their theme song tend to echo the following sentiments: "Who am I to judge? If someone else does something wrong, that is no business of mine. As long as things are good with me, everything is A-OK."

Of course, in such situations, everything is not A-OK. A bystander to a sea of wrong-doing gets wet. There is splash-back not only from what we do and say, but also from what we do *not* do and what we do *not* say. The privation from which Ignonos suffer is an almost total blindness to the fact that, like it or not, they are creating who it is they are becoming, even if they do nothing. Put simply, we are not only what we do, but *also* what we don't do. And what an adventure they are missing! They will find out, once they dive in, that although it sometimes requires deep, even agonizing, reflection, it is far more fun to attach to one's life than to "fun" times.

However, for any of us to see that our own lives matter, we sometimes need to borrow the perspective of others through questions that focus on how we are implicated in the tapestry of our interwoven lives.

On the other hand, we also need to remember that the opposite extreme of Ignono (i.e., the "busybody" who feels entitled to pontificate to all in her path) is likewise suffering from noxious splash back. Staying out may be the wrong thing to do in a situation, but it may be the right thing to do. Jumping in with both feet may be the wrong thing to do in a situation, but it may be the right thing to do. There is no rule book here, which is precisely why creating who we want to become requires thought at every step.

Questions to ask your kids

Q: Have you ever seen anyone throw trash on the ground? Did you say anything? Should you say something in that sort of situation?

Q: Have you ever thought that the clothes someone was wearing were ugly or weird or silly? If so, describe it. Did you say anything? Should you have said anything?

Q. Have you ever thought somebody's breath smelled bad? Did you say anything? Should you have said something?

Q. Have you ever seen someone at school treated unkindly? What happened? Did you do anything? Should you have done something?

Q. What could be the reason bystanders sometimes refrain from acting?

IGNOSTATUS

Ignostatuses are similar to Ignogreeds but differ in that they don't necessarily use "stuff" to mark their importance. They also differ from Ignotribus in that they are not overly concerned with the elevation of a particular group. These are individuals who are bent on showing everyone how cool they themselves are as individuals. They are frequently rebels without a cause, not realizing that rebellion for its own sake (i.e., without a cause) ensures that they are just as much ensnared by authority (whether that authority is a person or a group) as those who mindlessly conform. Examining what is perceived as "cool" frequently reveals that something is considered cool only, or primarily, because it differs from what has been (or is) the norm (e.g., black lipstick instead of red, pants with holes instead of without, etc.). However, precisely because what is cool becomes a norm of "cool," it too becomes the target against which the next generation of Ignostatuses will rebel. This is a short-lived status, but can be harmful if it is grounded in Ignome, or morphs into full-blown Ignotribus or Ignogreed.

Questions to ask your kids

Q. What is it you need to have in order to be cool? Think of examples in school or in your neighbourhood.

Q. What would be considered "uncool"? Why?

Q. Who decides what is cool? How does it change? How can you change it?

Q. Do you want to be cool? Why?

Q. Can something be (not) cool to some and not to others? Why?

Q. Can something be cool to everyone? Or nobody?

Activities

Ask your daddy/mommy/guardian who is the coolest? Why?

Draw something cool on one side of a piece of paper and something uncool on the other side. Without telling them what you think, ask your parents or friends which side they think is cool and which is uncool, and why. Now have your parents draw something that is cool and something that is uncool. Ask them to explain. Wonder together about how and why "coolness" has changed and wonder together about why people want to be cool.

IGNOFO

Ignofos differ from Ignostatuses in that, rather than wanting to stand out as special, they prefer to blend in. They don't aspire to be "cool." They aspire, rather, not to be "not cool." Even though these two are invariably together (all monarchs need subjects and vice versa), the character structure of the latter is fundamentally different from the former. Adorno spoke of the Ignofo as having an "authoritarian personality" in a book by that name.[8] Adorno, who escaped the Holocaust, was deeply perplexed by how it was possible that so many hitherto decent, well-meaning citizens could have come to celebrate the depravity of such an evil regime. The answer seemed to be that conforming to what we take to be an authority (whether it is a literal dictator or school mate) is a common trait in many of us. Hannah Arendt[9] famously referred to the "banality of evil," meaning that even the most mundane-seeming people, like Adolf Eichmann, can commit the most heinous crimes without much reflection, if they become a cog in the machine. And, in empirical support of this view, subsequent studies[10] showed that ordinary college students consented to shock and hence apparently harm what they thought was another college student, if they were ordered to do so by an authority figure. We all, then, run the danger of becoming a cog in the machine of our situated lives unless we remain vigilant.

So the challenge to us all is to be constantly on the alert to differentiating between benign conformity (since being rebellious for its own sake is simply jumping from the frying pan into the fire) and conformity that has the capacity to negatively define who we are.

Questions to ask your kids

Q. Do you know people at school who really try to fit in?

Q. How do they do that?

Q. Have you tried to fit in? Why?

Q. Why do people want to fit in?

Q. When is it ok to fit in? When not? Why?

Q. In what ways can trying to fit in be harmful?

Q. What would the world be like if we all fit in? What if nobody fit in?

Q. Is being different from most others a good thing? Why (not)?

Activity

Think about different cultures. Draw people from two different cultures on a sheet of paper. Now write down how they are different and how they are the same. Do these differences and/or similarities matter? How and why? Are some differences/similarities better than others?

Write down a list of ways you can try to fit in. See if you can make a matching drawing for each one of them. Order them according to effectiveness, then funniness and, finally, strangeness. Now think of other ways to order them for fun!

IGNOTRIBUS

We are all naturally inclined to form groups. It is built into our genes. Since all cooperative groups must protect themselves from exploitation, this requires the ability to distinguish Us from Them, as well as the tendency to favor Us over Them.[11] Studies have shown that even babies prefer their own kind.[12] Thus, the most natural reaction for any of us in meeting a stranger is fear, even hatred, rather than compassion. In this regard, we are like other primates. Jane Goodall in her book, *The Chimpanzees of Gombe*,[13] describes gangs of chimpanzees happening upon another tribe as follows: if there is a baby, they will kill and eat it; if there are females, they will rape them; if it is a male, they will mob him, rip his flesh from his body, bite off his toes and testicles, and leave him for dead.

Paul Bloom argues[14] that because of our in-born "coalitional nature," our biases are here to stay. But he goes on to say that we can use our intelligence to override our coalitional biases when we feel that they have started to run amok. After all, he adds "[j]ust as we have used reason to make scientific discoveries, such as the existence of dinosaurs, electrons, and germs, we have also used it to make moral discoveries, such as the wrongness of slavery."[15]

And so, by reasoning together, we may discover answers to such questions as whether we are justified in refusing to reach out to others because their language of origin is different, or because they belong to a different ethnic group, or because their skin is darker or lighter than our own. On the other hand, we might discover that other kinds of grouping are toxic—or perhaps somewhere in between. And that is precisely why we need reason to find our way.

Questions to ask your kids

Q. For non-immigrant youngsters: Is there anyone in your class that comes from a different country? Do you ever talk to them? Should you try to talk to them? Do you ever play with them? Should you try to play with them? Why (not)?

Q. For immigrant youngsters: Do you ever talk to kids who grew up in this country? Should you try to talk to them? Do you ever play with them? Should you try to play with them? Why (not)?

Q. Should children from other countries learn your language? Should you learn their language?

Q. What are some of things that you do best in school? Do you find that those of you who are good at the same thing tend to hang out together? Do you think you ever exclude anyone? Do you think that there is a problem if there is an exclusion? Why (not)?

Q. What kind of tribes do you see at school? Why are they tribes? How do you recognize them?

Q. Do you belong to any tribe?

Q. Can a tribe be based on clothes/jewelry/language/behaviour/etc.?

Q. Can tribes change? How? Why?

Activity

If you could start a tribe what kind of tribe would it be? Now design and make a flag that represents your tribe. Write down the constitution of your tribe, its characteristics and create an anthem. Now see if you can get others to join your tribe!

CONCLUSION

In the following experiment, 85 per cent of respondents said yes when asked "if someone sues you and loses, should that person pay the legal costs?" But when asked if they sued someone and lost, only 44 per cent said they should pay the other's legal costs.[16] And so it goes: our judgment is virtually always tainted, to some degree, by self-interest. But reason can make a huge difference here. It can help us to neutralize bias, and, in so doing, allow us to demonstrate to ourselves and others, that we are not simply a product of our inclinations and prejudices, but rather in control of the kind of people we are choosing to become.[17] This claim, that we are the captains of our own ships[18], is substantiated only if we can get as close as possible to viewing any given situation in an "impartial" way, and *that* requires that we reason with others and ourselves.

This does not, importantly, mean a rush to compromise. After all, should we have compromised with the Nazis? Should we have compromised with slave owners? Or, as Greene askes us: Should open-minded liberals fight for environmental regulations that are strong but not quite strong enough to stave off global warming?[19]

Rather than compromise, we ought to seek what we have in common with the other, and what we all have in common is our ability to reason. In that spirit, it is important for reasonable people to maintain a robust confidence that, despite its failures to always make in-roads, reason nonetheless is the most powerful weapon we have to overcome the many forces that create conflict and misery among us. And if reasonable people stay on the alert for the Igno forces that serve as obstacles to the possibility of "meeting in the *in-between*,"[20] our future, and the future of our children, will be one of which we are worthy.

1   Gardner, Susan T. "What Would Socrates Say to Mrs. Smith?" *Philosophy Now*. Issue 84. May/June 2011. 24-26.

2   Behary, Wendy T. *Disarming the Narcissist.* Harbinger, 2013.

3   Siegel, Daniel. *The Developing Mind.* The Guilford Press, 2012.

4   Bloom, Paul. *Just Babies*: *The Origins of Good and Evil.* Crown, 2013.

5   Norris, Trevor. *Consuming Schools: Commercialism and the End of Politics.* U of T, 2011.

6   Marcuse, Herbert. *The One Dimensional Man.* Beacon, 1964.

7   Henry, Wayne, Richard Morehouse, and Susan T. Gardner. "Combatting Consumer Madness." *Teaching Ethics, 2017*

8   Adorno, Theodor W, Else Frenkel-Brunswik, Daniel J. Levinson, Nevitt Sanford. *The Authoritarian Personality.* Harper, 1950.

9   Arendt, Hannah. *Eichmann in Jerusalem: A Report on the Banality of Evil.* Viking, 1963.

10 Milgram, Stanley. "Behavioral Study of Obedience." *Journal of Abnormal and Social Psychology*, 67, 1963, 371-378.

11 Greene, Joshua. *Moral Tribes.* Penguin, 2014.

12 Bloom.

13 Goodall, Jane. *The Chimpanzees of Gombe.* Belknap, 1986.

14 Bloom.

15 Bloom, 207.

16 Greene, 83.

17 Gardner, Susan T. *Thinking Your Way to Freedom*. Temple, 2009.

18 From the poem "Invictus."

19 Green, 336.

20 Buber, Martin. *I and Thou.* Free Press, 1971 (first published in German in 1923).

CPSIA information can be obtained
at www.ICGtesting.com
Printed in the USA
LVHW07s0548170518
577473LV00005B/5/P

9 781525 514777